BOULDERS

LIFE WITH PARKINSON'S DISEASE

Stories by Steven Briggs
Edited by Anthony Lyle
Illustrations by Steven Briggs

authorHOUSE®

AuthorHouse™
1663 Liberty Drive
Bloomington, IN 47403
www.authorhouse.com
Phone: 1 (800) 839-8640

Published by AuthorHouse   05/12/2015

ISBN: 978-1-5049-0674-6 (sc)
ISBN: 978-1-5049-0675-3 (e)

Library of Congress Control Number: 2015905832

Print information available on the last page.

CONTENTS

FOREWORD

I first met Steve in the apartment complex where we both lived. At that time, his Parkinson's was not noticeable although he had already been diagnosed. His wife and mine passed away within a few months of each other. We started going to breakfast together every weekend.

Over the years, I was witness to his body's continual process of degrading due to his illness' (along with Parkinson's, he also experiences Scoliosis and Osteo-arthritis). While his body deteriorates, his mind is completely intact. He has continued to maintain his dignity and his sense of humor. This work of his is an attempt to help people understand life with Parkinson's (both those who have just been diagnosed and those who never will have it).

He didn't quit because of his growing disabilities from complications of PD. He continued to work at his job and didn't want to retire when he was long overdue to do so. Even after retiring, he continued to volunteer at the USDA Forest Service, RMRS Shrub Sciences Laboratory in Provo, Utah, refusing to "throw in the towel". I hope this work encourages others diagnosed with PD to do the same.

It was my pleasure to be able to edit his work. While his mind is intact, his spelling and grammar is atrocious! I hope that you find this work helpful in understanding what life is like for a person who has Parkinson's.

INTRODUCTION

I have been diagnosed with having Parkinson's (PD). Did you catch that? I said I was "diagnosed" with having PD. The only way to be certain that one has PD is by doing a brain autopsy. I ain't dead yet!!!!!!!!!!!

The best ways to treat PD are with continuing education and laughter. Laughter is probably the most important medication. I was diagnosed with having PD in 2009, with symptoms first appearing in 2007. I started fighting from day one by reading as much as possible, and there seems to have been an explosion of information. At first, I only told those people who need to know, then I decided that I had nothing to be ashamed of, I had a non-contagious disease. They had nothing to fear.

I read somewhere, that a person has PD but the PD doesn't have them, I adopted this as my philosophy and to have a positive attitude. I told my co-workers that I planned on working another five years, maybe 10, little did I know of the changes that lay ahead!

My wife died in 2012, Scoliosis and Osteo-arthritis, made their presence known in 2013. I retired in January 2014, with 40+ years of Federal service. The battle continues. Life has always been a rocky road, now the rocks are larger, hence the title "Boulders". We still can get around then. So, it is my hope that with these stories that the road of life will be a little straighter and less bumpy for all. To my readers, care partners, and all others, in the words of Roy Rogers: *HAPPY TRAILS TO YOU...*

Introduction to Our Character

We don't know a lot about my character (sometimes me, other times purely fictional, any resemblance to any other person, is coincidental). He is 65, grew up in the mid-west with patriotic parents. Graduated from high school (just) and worked the summer in the local malt shoppe before joining the Navy. He owns his own home (well almost), married his high school sweetheart and has three sons. He is either retired or on disability. He loves life, and Parkinson's one rock, he makes the best of it.

/s/ Steven Briggs, March 2015

DEDICATION

These stories are dedicated to those with Parkinson's, their care givers/partners, their families, and loved ones. To Doctors, Researchers, and all the rest that are in some way involved with Parkinson's. THANK YOU!

Chapter 1: A TYPICAL DAY

Let me tell you what a typical day is like for me, "A Person with Parkinson's (PWP) Disease". First, after the shock of the news that you are a PWP, and all that goes with the diagnosis, doctors tell us to get lots of exercise, we already get more than we may realize, for example:

SHUTTING OFF THE ALARM: Reach out, move arm up and down until you find the button. Of course many people take the same exercise without PD too, but it's a little more complicated with PD. By the time I find the $@^$ arlarm, my heart is pumping hard!

TURNING ON THE BED SIDE LAMP: Move hand back and forth, slowly. Once the lamp is found move hand to switch.

GETTING OUT OF BED: Sit up, swing feet out until the floor is found. Add accessories as needed (Teeth, glasses, hearing aid, find slippers (what are they doing over there??)) Whew, exhausted already!

NEXT: The Parkinson shuffle. Uh-oh, double time, thank goodness for adult under pants.

GETTING DRESSED:

SOCKS: Sit on bed, grab sock, and roll on to your back. Bend knee bringing foot towards out stretched arms with the sock. Slip on sock (if it hangs up, time for a pedicure). Pull towards heel, then up, stretch leg out while wiggling toes. Aahh good. Repeat OTHER side. Then take a break to get your wind!

PANTS: Retrieve from chair, holding by the waist, shake out until the legs are next to each other? (Repeat as necessary). Insert foot and hop twice. Sit down and pull pant leg over the foot. Repeat other side and STAY SEATED!! Now stand, pulling pants up while wiggling hips. (Thank Goodness for elastic!)

T-SHIRTS: Ever notice that you have to put them on twice? You stick one arm in, then the other, and pull over your head, only to find it's backwards? Okay, I know, I know... This is true for most people but it's frustrating when you have to do calisthenics to get dressed. Couldn't find the front because it's one of these new tag less shirts! Then you have to get someone to pull it down in back, because you can't reach it.

Button shirts? FORGET THEM!! You can get them on easily enough, but the buttons or holes (or both) are too small, and someone has to help you.

SHOES: Where did I take them off? AHH, here they are, the brown "Hush Puppies", they go good with everything, except for green socks!

Well that's the end of our morning exercise program, only took us 45 minutes. Whewww. Time for a shower and a nap?

MENTAL ACTIVITY:

Now, to keep us mentally sharp, doctors have us counting pills. Let's start with the little red pill, for Parkinson's. It controls tremors, 3 per day. Then there's the little white, for Parkinson's. It helps red pill, twice a day. Next the yellow pill, for high cholesterol, twice a day. Keeping on with the colors, the blue and white, for Parkinson's, once a day (too pretty to take). The brown pill is for BPH, once a day. Ah! The brown with black stripes pill is for BPH and also once a day, complements the other brown pill. The white oval pill is for hypertension (which calms you after trying to get dressed) is once a day. The big white pill is next. I forget what it's for, but something the doctor wants me to take. Not done yet! The other big white pill, something the wife wants me to take. (Should I be worried?) The blue pill is for... hummm. Hea-yea!! In case she doesn't have a headache tonight! Keeping all that straight is a rigorous mental exercise!

Recreation is a big part of my day and just as important as physical exercise. My recreation program includes the following:

BREAKFAST: Bran cereal, milk, whole wheat, dry toast with jam or jelly on the side, and orange juice. The doctor removed coffee from the menu. On the weekends, I meet the boys at the local diner. Boys? Hardly! I'm the youngest at 65.

NAP TIME: Dang cat, get out of MY recliner!

LUNCH TIME: Meals on wheels or as I call it "truck-n-grub"!

After all that, I'm ready to relax some!

TV TIME: let's see what is on:
World Cup Soccer (WCS)
NFL football
WCS
NBA

WCS

NHL Highlights

WCS

NCAA Football

WCS

MLB: FINALLY!! Game 2 of Division leaders of a 3 game series. Dang it! I wanted to watch the CUBS! My favorite team. What ever happened to "American as Baseball, apple pie, and Chevrolet!"? Now it's World Cup Soccer, Greek yogurt, and Honda or is it Hyundai??

So much for TV, think I'll go for a long walk. Now where is my walker? HUFFING! Made it to the end of the block, but George passed me. He has a new wheeled walker. NO FAIR! I'd better get one with a motor, if I'm going to pass him. Think I'll take a nap. (It's OK to take naps when you have PD.)

DINNER TIME: Always a surprise. The wife is still a good cook, even with left overs.

TV TIME again: OH-Boy, a Gene Autry western! They don't make them like this anymore.

BED TIME: Going from street clothes to PJ's, it takes 20 minutes.

Well, that pretty much sums up my day, guess I need a hobby or two so I'm not spending so much time in front of the TV. Maybe gardening?
OOH, what's this!!? The BLUE PILL.
I'm going to get lucky tonight!

Chapter 2: GROCERY SHOPPING

With shopping list in hand, I give the Missis a peck good-bye. "Now stick to the list, no extras like last time!" She yells as I get in the car. "Yes dear", I mumble. I always get the last word at least.

Arriving at the store, I see that all the "Handicapped" spaces are taken. Must be "Senior Day". I think, "aaaah"! Here is a spot. Get between the lines?? Yep, we won't count the one the tires are resting on. Better put up the "Handicapped" permit, so they know what kind of idiot parked this way.

It's a long way to the store. Oh well, Doc says I need to walk more. Better get a cart. Big or little? Better get a big one. With a long list, it's faster than my walker. Grab the cane. Another one of these "Republican" carts, (pulls to the right). I'll exchange it when we get inside. That's better, now to the list.

MILK. Why do they always put it at the back of the store?? Young Man! Young Man! Ooh excuse me, Miss. Do you work here? Could you please get me a half gallon of whole milk? Thank you. Why don't they put the half gallons in the middle for us shorter people? Pretty little filly, where was she 45 years ago? Well....., come to think on it, the Missis wasn't so bad. Got three fine sons, now I'm the old sway back plow horse. NOW, back to the list!

EGGS: (make sure they aren't cracked). If I did that they would be scrambled before I got them into the cart. Hummm. A new product? Crack-n-Heat! Will have to think about that one.

ORANGE JUICE: (the wife keeps reminding me to read labels). "Shake well"! No problem there. Don't even have to try.

WHEAT CRACKERS: "Contains wheat". DUH! That's why the call them "Wheat" crackers. I wonder. Do chocolate bars say "contains chocolate"? I'll have to go look.

NUTRITIONAL DRINKS (or as I call them: Pop-n-slop): They do make a good lunch when the wife is off playing Bridge. Better get some straws, the kind that bend at the top. Nutritional drinks do not look well on my sweater. Better warn your friends about accepting sodas fetched by you. Nasty surprise when they open em up.

APPLES: So many varieties; Red delicious, Golden delicious, Gala, Jazz, Granny Smith, Fiji! Which ones to get? Hummm...., I know, I'll get one of each. The checker will love me for that!!

FROZEN PEAS: Use to be able to eat then with a knife. Now I use a spoon (big one) and they still fall off! By the time I get them to my mouth, I'm lucky one is left on the spoon. I once saw my friend reaching out to help me keep my scrambled eggs on my fork, but he managed to stop himself. It's a tough call sometimes. Do you help or do you let me spill my food on my own?

Make sure you lean over the plate. At least that way the food eventually gets eaten anyway.

ICE CREAM: (NO, mint chocolate chip), my favorite. Vanilla again.

KETCHUP: (or is it CATSUP?) Here it is! Ohh Lordy!!! A whole section where they put the labels on upside down! Wife wants 32oz. I'll get 64, last twice as long. EXPIRES in three days? I never have known the stuff to go bad.

HAMBURGER: Get 1 POUND? Humm. Let's see: 1.85, 1.65, 1.35, or 1.15. I'll get the 1.65 package. That way we'll have 1 pound of actually cooked meat.

INSTANT POTATOES: I'll get the cheap stuff. They all taste the same.

APPLE SAUCE: More soft food? I CAN chew (when I put my teeth in).

Well, that's it!! Now to check out. I wonder if May is working today? She likes me.

As I unload the cart, I'm asked "is that all"? I should hope so!! "PAPER or PLASTIC"? Better make it plastic, they have handles. DARN! Left the canvas bags at home again! Not too heavy. "CUSTOMER CARD"? Oh yes, let's see; drug store, other grocery store, other drug store, department store, third drug store, nope don't have one. Phone number? 123-555-2396. "CASH, CREDIT, or DEBIT"? Cash!! Not fast enough to push the buttons in time to do cards. "HELP TO THE CAR"? Two more and we can play 20 questions!!!

Aaah, home at last! Now to get them in the house! I didn't see any of the neighbor kids. Hope I can get groceries in before the ice cream melts. Doc's other exercise program. Carry in/ put away; step up, stretch, (hold on to cabinet) step down, bend over, stand up. REPEAT until done.

FINALLY! NAP TIMEzzzzzzzzzzzzz.

Chapter 3: GARDENING
A SEASON LONG ADVENTURE

Aah! SPRING! At least according to that furry rodent back in Pennsylvania! Daffodils and crocus are up. Better put on the rubber boots (Wellington's). It looks a little muddy. In a week the garden area will be bone dry.

Let's see what shall we plant this year? Marigolds? Helps to keep the bugs away, or so I'm told. Petunias? I like petunias but what color? Think I'll go patriotic this year; red, white and blue.

Vegetables; radishes, green beans, corn, peas. Aah! Better make a list getting a little forgetful these days. Ooops! Forgot to take the boots off! Now I have to mop the floor. (Two hours later). Let's see, that should just about do it. To the nursery!

"Oh sir, can you direct me to the seeds? Grass or vegetables"? Vegetables. I have enough grass. Of course it's mostly crab. Better get a cart. Will need it for the flowers. Oh No!! Not another political one! Pulls left this time. I bet the next one will go around in circles. And no it's not ME!

Green beans: snap, wax, string, bush or vine? GEE! Decisions, decisions! Guess I'll get the vine type. But I'll have to build a trellis for the peas. Might as well continue it for the beans. Less bending over at harvest time too. Hardiness zones? If they ain't hardy for here, why sale them?

Planting: Let's see. We'll plant the petunias at the far end; a red, white, and blue border. The marigold's at this end with a gap to walk in. Hard to step over any more. Corn and pumpkins will go over there, and the peas and beans over there. And better get the string. Otherwise my row will look like the Mississippi River.

Well that's enough for today! Lunch! Then a nap! Dang cat! In MY recliner, again!

Back to the garden; three seeds per mound. Now there's a challenge. Try that with PD! Let's see. That one has four, that one two and that one five. By the time I get done it will be close to three. "Shake seeds into quarter in deep straight line"! Right! Who ever heard of a person with Parkinson's doing anything straight? I'll be lucky to get even close! Finally, all done, now to sit back and watch everything grow.

BIRDS! Where is that cat now?! Asleep in MY recliner again! I'll get him this time (got one of them power lift kind), remote up. Ha, got ya! Now go out and chase those birds.

Did I say "watch <u>everything</u> grow"? Them weeds are growing pretty good. Better get the cultivator and kneeler/seat. Nifty little thing. It has handles on it to help you get up (I can use all the help I can get, these days), or turn it over and it's a seat.

Beans and peas are looking good. Got ya!, thought you sneak past me! On to the next one. Grandma taught me to remove all of the weed. That way you are not weeding it twice. Better thin the radishes. The row is only six inches wide this year. Not bad. One year they were two feet from the line. The new pills helping? Oops, I'd better pull the weeds or I won't have any left.

Lunch time/nap time! Aah all weeded. And time to start over again.

Corn is lookin' good. "Knee high by the Fourth of July". Them Iowa farmers say we should be there. Got a couple of pumpkins coming too. Will need to raise them up and put some cardboard underneath. It helps to keep them round.

Fine crop this year! No bugs. Oh some leaf cutters on the beans and rhubarb, but nothing that I needed to spray for. Guess I can call them "organic" this year. Plenty for us and to donate too. Water, fertilizer and LOVE, that's how my garden grows! Did I mention the LOVE comes with some tough love and a few words that I don't let my wife hear?

The first hard frost. The end of another season. Pile up everything in the corner for composting. The marigolds and petunias were great this year. Think I'll plant some daisies too. Maybe I'll have my neighbor Ben build me a couple of raised beds, next year? Less bending over.

Day is done! Laying back in my recliner with the cat on my lap a purring. Watching a Randolph Scott western. What a way to end the day? The cat didn't do too bad of a job keeping the birds out. Think he had fun doing it. Think I'll keep him around.

Chapter 4: BATHING/SHOWERING

NO! NO! I'm not promoting that you shower with a friend! Although the last time that me and the Missis did it, it was fun!!

Now to the story. Dressed in my new comfy Terri-cloth robe, slippers on, I head for the bathroom (water closet, for you military folks). Why I wear the slippers, I don't know. It's carpet all the way and it's only 20 feet. Guess, I always have and always will. Less I forget. Let's see, do

I have everything I need; Soap on a rope, Help button, Dog Tags, (haven't hardly ever taken them off in fifty years). (Any more stuff around the neck and I'll look like that actor: "Mr. T".), Shampoo, Hair conditioner (don't know why, ain't got much left), Nail brush (gotta git the garden dirt from under the nails), Small scrub brush (gotta have clean hands for Sunday, otherwise people will think you have been working before church), Long handle scrub brush (huummm, I wonder what happened to those door to door salesmen?), Bath chair (in case I get tired), Grab bars (had them installed a year ago. It is reported that one in three people over 65 fall in the tub (I plan on falling out)), Non-skid strips (one half foot apart, one strip under the ball, the other under the heel. Half a foot!) Did I get the Help Button? Think that's everything. I need to make a check list. Oh darn! Face cloth and towel.

Water--not too hot, not too cold-----aaah! Forgot to turn the handle down for the shower head. Boy is that water cold! Careful getting in and out. Fall and break a hip and the missis said she would just shoot me. I'm sure she was just kidding... (nervous laughter here).

Aah. Now for a relaxing bath /shower. Do a little of both. Flip the lever and let the tub fill. Feels good to soak the feet.

Rub-a-dub, rub-a-dub, three men in a tub, rub-a-dub... How does the rest of it go? I read somewhere that there was some off-color meaning to these ol rhymes. Oh well, I can't remember, rub-a-dub, three people in a tub! (Gotta be politically correct). Oh yeah, the butcher, the baker, and the candle stick maker! (An odd lot) Rub-a-dub three people in the tub.

Soap up, rinse, soap up, rinse, that's the Navy way. OH NO!! I dropped the shampoo bottle! Just missed the foot too! Good thing it is a plastic bottle! Still would've hurt plenty. Slowly slide down holding the grab bar, bend the knees, keep the back straight. Gotch ya! Slippery little devil.

Rub-a dub, three men in a tub. Time to get out. Beginning to look like a prune, but to be truthful, I was half way there when I got in. Flip the lever again, and away go troubles go down the drain. Still remember that ol jingle! Nice thought.

Remember back in the day when we did the "twist" to dry our backs? With PD, we can let the tremors do the work without all the energy. And with these new towels, we can wrap myself up to get to the places I can't reach and still have some for the face and hair.

Let's see how we did. Finger nails, clean. Check. Hands, clean, huummm. Maybe I'd better shave. The good old electric shaver is good for a quick job. Better brush my teeth while I'm here. Now where did I leave them? On the night stand, of course! Clean body, clean clothes, ready to tackle the world, to the garden! Oops! Church! Alleluia!

Chapter 5: HOME MAINTENANCE AND SAFETY

    I recently purchased a "help button" because my family members were concerned that I might fall and no one would find me, since I live alone (this was after the misses passed, God rest her soul). Soo.., I got one. Hope they are happy now! I have been doing other things to make it safer for me, let's go down the list.

TRIPPING HAZARDS: Since falling is a leading cause of injury and death of people with Parkinson's (PD), I thought I would start out here. Got me several rolls of that double-sided sticky tape for the throw rugs. Doesn't last very long. Especially when the cat goes racing around the corners after who knows what. Don't understand cats. Anyhow, I put a square on each corner, does help keep them in place for a little while? That's why I bought two rolls.

Then, I looked at my extension cords and made sure none of them crossed a door or hall. I taped them together to make them look neater. Huummm. That one is beginning to look like ol what's his name. You know that fellow in that 1950's Christmas movie. The one who is blowing the fuses all the time. Anyhow I'd better check to see if I need all of them. Don't put them under the throw rugs neither.

Put a bell on the cat's collar. He always seemed to be under my feet after he finished a nap. He wants food or petting. Gives the birds an advantage. Sometimes they seem to play a game with the cat.

Pick up your clothes and put them in a hamper. They can get caught between the toes and trip you up as easy as anything else. Papers too! They can be slippery, even on carpet.

FALLING HAZARDS: Bought myself a new step ladder for the kitchen, the kind that has a high handle on it so I can steady myself when I reach for the top shelf. You still have to be careful. If you lean too far to the side you can still tip over! And hope that you don't get the shakes!

ELECTRICIAL MAINTENANCE: Hired an electrician. Talk about plumbers being expensive! Electricians ain't cheap either! Anyhow I'd had him install motion detector switches. Lots of choices in what they can do. I just got the simple ones (Some of them you need a college degree to operate) in the front hall, bathroom, and the back stairs. Sure is nice to have the lights come on when you got your hands full. Had to have him come back and adjust them. The cat thought it was great fun to turn the lights on and off by passing across the sensor. Put in some lighted switches too. They help navigate at night when headed for the refrigerator. Checked the outlets. Didn't need all those extension cords.

All the rest of the wiring is good. WHOO-EEE, don't ask an Electrician to change a light bulb. You'd thought the world was coming to an end.

Those 48 inch fluorescent tubes are somehow to go into a cabinet that is 47 and 7/8 inches. Ooh the marvels of the modern world! Need that degree in engineering now. Anyhow he got them in lick-it-split, he must know some tricks of the trade. He should for what he charges!

PLUMBING MAINTENANCE: Had a plumber come over. Good shape there! The "J" pipes under the sinks had been changed to plastic a couple of years ago. They don't wear out like the chrome ones do. Put in a single lever kitchen faucet. Got one with a spray nozzle. Makes it easier when cleaning the big stuff. He also put in a couple of "ball" valves, quarter turn on and off. Will make it nice for the next person who has to tinker under there.

Nice fellow, gave me a list of things to watch for and things that will need to be done soon. Replace the water heater in five years or so and they will be more energy efficient by that time. Recommended single lever faucets for the bathroom sink and shower. Also to get the kind that the shower head that can go up and down. He also gave me a card for a Lady to come over to make recommendations on making the bathroom

"ADA compliant". Not sure what that is, but I'll give her a call.

I also had the city power department come out, and they did a 15 point inspection of the house, inside and out. Not too much money, and I can get a rebate! That's money back, when I do some of the things they recommended. Will help make the place more comfy too.

STAIRS: Stairs both inside and out can be a major safety concern!! They seem to attract toys and other stuff faster than you can pick them up. My mother used them as a sorter for the mail, "Important Mail" (Bills and Letters, back in the days when people wrote letters) on one step, magazines on another, and "junk mail" (yep, we called it that even back then) on the next. Too bad we don't have a junk mail mailbox, one that automatically eats the mail and spits out some kind of compost. It would be about the same quality as manure!

Anyhow, you want to keep the stairs free of "stuff" (like that word – Like George Carlin said, my stuff and your junk). You will want handrails on both sides and use them! Be sure they are the proper height, and well anchored to hold your weight. Carpet or runners must be firmly affixed to the stairs. NEVER use throw rugs!

Good lighting is a must for all stairs, inside and out. Basement stairs are notorious for being dark (watch any good horror flick). Outside basement stairs usually only have a single 25 watt bulb above the door. Front doors aren't much better. You have more light, but rarely is there adequate light on the stairs. Stairs and hallways should have three way switches (the kind that let you turn on the lights from either end). Use them!! That's what they are there for!

If stairs are still a problem, consider putting your bedroom on the main floor. If that is not possible, a personal elevator or whatever they call the ones you put in the stair wells might work for you. Remember, if you get one of these, everyone will want to ride it at first.

There is so much more to say about stairs. I could go on for several more pages and still leave something out. Consider snow and ice, leaves and rain, and nonskid material on painted areas. Ramps can be expensive, one foot of length for every inch up and it may require special permission from the city.

HOUSE AND YARD INSPECTION: Inspected the house and yard myself. Been here near thirty years. I will pay it off in another six months. Let's see; handrails tight, CHECK. Garden hose rolled up, CHECK (humm, need a little paint there). Outlet covers in place, CHECK. Bushes trimmed, lawn mowed, and leaves raked. Johnny does a good job with those chores.

Did you know that wet leaves on the sidewalk can be slippery as ice? Speaking of ice, Johnny is snow shoveling wizard. Johnny will be out two or three times during a storm, and when the storm is over, I have the cleanest sidewalks in the neighborhood, next to Johnny's of course.

Oh, Johnny, he is my neighbor's boy, real hard worker! Figures it's easier to lift two inches of snow three times than six inches once and it is easier to walk through two inches than six. Loves a cup of good hot chocolate too. Johnny keeps salt and sand on the walks then the snow melts. Like I said, a hard worker and all around good kid.

YEP, that should just about do it, probably think of something else later, always do, well I just have to add it to the list for next year.

Just wanted to say that Home Maintenance, Safety, and Good Housekeeping all go hand-in-hand. Reduce the risk of falling and helps keep the value in the place you worked for so long and hard. Six more months!

Chapter 6: GOING OUT TO EAT

"To go out or not to go out. That is a darn good question! Whether tis nobler to suffer the slings and arrows of outrageous mishaps while going out or to sleep in and eat at home....Ah to sleep. Perchance to dream of days gone by when I was young and strong." by William Shakespeare (sort of). Had to add a little culture, if these are not Shakespeare's words, they certainly are inspired by him.

I've been invited out to eat! Alarm! Alarm!! Ringing, ringing!! Panic, Panic!! Emergency, Emergency Will Robbins... or something like that. Sorry if you don't know the ol TV shows, this one was from Lost in Space.

Where we going?? Fancy or causal? What to wear? Do I need a tie? HELLLPP!

Relax, I tell myself. Call your friends back and find out what they have in mind. Then go from there.

Aaah, causal! The last time I wore a tie, it got into everything; salad, mashed-potatoes and gravy, and even the green beans! And try to tie one of those things with hands that shake around like a vibrator.

At the restaurant, we are promptly greeted. Nice! Table or booth? "Do the chairs have arms"? Better take the booth! I can discreetly sit straighter in a chair with arms but in booths, I'm somewhat hidden. With the scoliosis, I tend to lean heavily and the wall helps to hold me up. My friend mentioned that someday he'll have to eat under the table with me. Smart @^@#$. Still he's a good guy.

Napkin? Tuck it in the collar or lap? Lap, we're in public. Now, where do I put my cane? Aah good! There is a hook on the end of the booth, just don't forget it, like I did in Montana.

Nice place. Today I get waited on, instead of everyone waiting on me. Can the kitchen cut my steak into bite size pieces? Kind of embarrassing to have some reach over and cut my meat like a youngster. Some steaks are so tough you need a power saw. Must have been taken from a range steer raised in Wyoming. Everything is tough in Wyoming. Have you seen the grazing lands there? Even jackrabbits and jackelopes carry canteens! At least in the southern part, some of Wyoming is quite beautiful.

Back to the meal, the travelogue will be another story. The baked potato is huge! Must be from Idaho. They know how to grow potatoes there. Mixed vegetables? I really don't like them, but eat them anyway. Desert? Cherry pie, please. Cherry is as American as apple, besides, didn't George cut down a cherry tree?

Good meal, good friends, good conversation! AND I don't have to pay for it. I'll leave a little for the tip. I had a real nice waitress, severed us....er... I mean served us without asking who got what and kept our drinks full. Even the manager came by to ask about our meals.

Home again, with a full stomach. Time for a Randolph Scott western and a nap in MY recliner. DAMNED cat!!

Chapter 7: A VISIT TO THE DOCTOR'S OFFICE

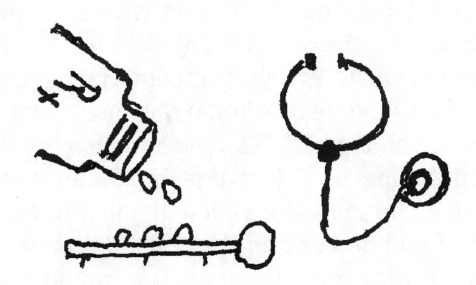

Off to the Doctor's office. Whoooheee! Got an early appointment. If you get there later than 10, your waiting time grows exponentially with every hour after 10. I once woke up and the lights were off. Okay, that's not quite true!

Shouldn't have to wait this time. Humm, all of the handicapped spots are filled. Drat. Ahh, here's a spot and it is closer than some of the Handicapped spaces.

Doc's office is on the fourth floor, these elevators have got to be the slowest in town! Wait, I know that tune... from 1936 I think. Bet ya, I could take the stairs and beat them! Not today. Made it just in time. You know a person with Parkinson's can be late for anything, except for Doctor's appointments. I read that somewhere. How true! To the author: Thank You!!

"Please sign in", wasn't that part of a game show in the 50's? Oh Yea, "What's My Line". "Has your insurance changed?" "Is your address correct?" I should hope so. I just left it 20 minutes ago. "You need to sign the yellow highlighted areas, two on front and one on the back." (You can't get blood out of a turn-up, as my Dad would say).

"Thank you, the Doctor will be right with you." Right, I mumble as I look for a spot to sit. That's a fib if ever I heard one!

The waiting room is nearly full already! At least no one is coughing. Here's a chair in the corner with a copy of 'Sports Illustrated' on the table. Shucks, no swimsuit edition. Not that it would do me much good without my blue pill. Haven't look at one of these since the last time I was here. Think it might be the same one.

The nurse calls my name, just as I was ready to fall asleep. I follow her down the hall to the very last exam room. Glad I brought my cane.

"Now, we'll take a few vitals", she informs me. Weight? I just lost five pounds on the hike to here to the office! Part of Doc's secret exercise program. Not too bad. At least I'm not getting fat with the wife's cooking. Blood Pressure? A little high after that walk! She writes it down and takes my temperature. She sticks the machine in my ear. Better than trying to hold a thermometer under my tongue for five minutes and try to answer their questions! And better still up the you know what! "Normal" she says. "The doctor will be right with you," as she closes the door. Right. Where have I heard that before? Oh right, about an hour ago.

Well, let's see what there is in here to read? 'Ladies Home Journal, September 1999', 'Time, July 2008,' and they claim that people are stealing magazines out of doctor's offices. A knock on the door.

"Hi, I'm Randy, Doc's PA," PA?? What in the #*@& is a PA?? I'm a Physicians Assistant. I screen patients before the doc sees them. Screen them for what? The shakes?

"Hop up on the table." What am I, a rabbit? Let's take your blood pressure, he has the cuff around my arm before he has finished his question. The nurse just did this a half an hour ago! Again he writes it down without saying anything. "Let's check your reflexes." The little rubber hammer to the knee, huh? Almost got him! "Very good, I'll get the Doc. He'll be right with you." HA! OH Randy, what was my blood pressure? "121 over 72, normal."

He closes the door. That's about what I had at home. Doc want me to keep my blood pressure under control, but they won't tell you the numbers. How can you keep it in control when they won't tell you the numbers?? (Another hour?)

Knock on the door, "Come in." "Hi Doc." Finally! I get to see the doc. We run through the usual questions. How are you? How's the hearing? "WHAT?" I answer and we both laugh. Blood pressure is good. How's the Parkinson's? "Good, I guess. No tremors that I notice, the pills seem to be working." "Good, we'll see you in four months. Randy, walk him up front to make the appointment". Two hour appointment and only

10 minutes of that was with the doctor. Hmmm Something is wrong with this picture.

"Hi Julie." "How's Monday the 27th at 10 a.m.?" "Good." "We'll see you then, here's your reminder card." Oh goody, another card for the "Philco." Need to clean them off, some are at least two years old. "Did you see Kathy? She needs to draw some blood." Kathy is good, all you ever feel is a pin prick. Wish I could take her to the hospital, those folks poke and poke, never seem to find the vein and you wind up with bruises on both arms.

Let's see, just over two hours, but it seemed a lot longer. Should be out to the car in 15 minutes. Good thing the building isn't any taller. Otherwise they would have to provide lunch. Oh-no! Another 'truck-n-grub' meal!! LORD, make the elevator go faster!

Chapter 8: HOBBIES

Everyone needs an indoor hobby, right? Can't garden when it's raining. Well, I have one as well. I have a small train set (kind-of always liked trains) that I put together over the years, fortunately most it before my PD took hold. It's a nice layout with a small village as the center focus and still has room to grow. I've had it for a while. Often, it was a nice catch place for my mail, bills, and dust.

Later, as my PD got worse, it became harder to work on, but not impossible. I just need more patience, as if I didn't need patience when I COULD work on the layout.

Having hobbies that need still hands can be hard. Steady hands at that. Yet, I still find it helps, and sometimes I find other ways (who says you can't teach an old dog new tricks).

Train collectors often have shows and I like to go to the shows. There's one in the big city about twice a year at the Convention Centre (don't know why they spell it that way). I have a friend that goes with me to the train show. He won't let me drive. Something about the way I drive scares him. I'm not sure I get it, except that he says he followed me once and he said I used 3 lanes... at once.

Sometimes it's funny, but when he meets me for breakfast and uses flashlights with the little orange extensions to help guide me into a parking space... it's almost not funny. Okay, that was funny too, once. Sometimes he doesn't park so straight either!!! He's deaf, so my muttering of names goes unnoticed.

Still it's nice to have a friend drive me to the train shows. I have to admit, I don't hear nearly as many cars honking as we drive. And when people wave, they use ALL of their fingers. I'm sure it's only because they don't know about my disabilities. If they did, ... well they still might use one finger waves. The misses says my bad driving has nothing to do with P.D. Right!

Once the train is set up, it's fairly easy to watch the trains go around (never did figure out how to wire the switches) and hope that one of them doesn't derail. Getting that sucker back on the tracks can be... well difficult at best and *&%$# at other times.

Well, it's my railroad, and I enjoy it! The missis ask when I'm going to finish. Well, as any good railroader knows, as I put my engineer's cap on, it's never finished. *"I've been working on the railroad all day long......"*

Chapter 9: ROAD TRIP/TRAVEL LOGUE

"...on the road again
Going places that I've never been
Seein' things that I may never see again
And I can't wait to get on the road again"

(lyrics and music by willie Nelson)

Aah nobody can sing it like Willie Nelson!
Will be picking my youngest boy, Patrick (Not Pat or Pattie), soon. He's going to school. I mean college, up in Idaho. Doing quite well too. We're going back to Illinois to visit Grandma and see some of this country that you don't see from

a jet plane (another song I like). Quality time together, I hope.

Yellowstone, the grand-dad of all the National Parks. Haven't been here since the fall of '90, two years after the fires. And my first time in the west entrance. Got a senior pass! Cost half as much and good at the other parks too.

Passed a solar powered caution sign, "buffalo," a little bit ago. BOING, BOING!! A deer crosses the road. Funny looking "Buffalo." Not the way I remember buffalo looking at all!

Hey did you hear about the young adult (politically correct) that wanted to move the deer crossing sign because too many deer were getting killed at the crossing? No?

Forest coming back nicely. Huumm, this area planted and this reseeded. I thought it was supposed too come back naturally. Must have their reasons. Right or left? Left. Getting close to lunch. Better stop here. Not much till Cody.

Patrick drove from the west entrance till we stopped for lunch and I drove the rest of the day. After lunch, we cross "Fishing Bridge," "NO FISHING FROM BRIDGE." HUMM... As we continue east, I think Patrick doesn't like mountain driving. Me neither. Getting to be a bit of a 'flat lander.' I'm glad it's late summer. Not much traffic.

Rodeo in Cody tonight. Not going to find a room here! (We're moteling this trip, so no tales of putting the tent up in the rain or wind. That's a book in itself! No tales of fixing hot chocolate on cold frosty mornings. I find hot chocolate warms the inside better than coffee). We'll push on for another hour or so. Looks to be good farmin' country, not like the southern part of the state. Another mountain range to cross, then we pick up the Interstate near Buffalo and on to South Dakota!

Lunch in Spearfish. I drive to Mount Rushmore. Gone are the "pig tails". Probably couldn't get the motor Homes under the bridges. (Motor home, humm? They are big as a "Greyhound" bus, and bigger than some apartments, and all you need is a driver's license!). The Park is free, but parking $10.00. That's the way they gitcha. I find a 'Handicapped' parking spot near the entrance. We walk the Avenue of Flags and view the sculptures. Do you want to see the movie? We go through the gift shop and we leave with no souvenirs. They tore down the 'A' frame visitor center (remember the movie: "North by Northwest"). I felt that it was as much a part of the Park as the sculptures. They didn't ask me! Oh well.

Uh-oh, I've locked the keys in the car! Let's see, yep I got the cell phone (just got one of those flip phones, the buttons are bigger and I don't need all of that other stuff). Let's see what is the triple A number. How long will it take them to get here?? Oh good, Patrick has the spare key. Back on the road again. Drove by 'Wall Drug'! Takes up the whole block now, lots of parking too.

Goofed again, Badlands National Monument was only four miles down the road. We could have driven through part of it without any loss of time! Patrick didn't seem to care.

Time to start looking for a place to put up for the night. The car in front of us exits. Hope they don't get the last room. We get to the edge of town, two abandoned gas stations. They turn around. I drive into a typical mid-western farming community, feed store, tractor supply, small grocery store, cafe (where the unofficial town council meets on Saturday morning), and the Post Office. Two exits later we find a place, have a late dinner at the cafe next door. Looked like they were getting ready to close.

Got up early, if you call 8 A.M. early. Grab a cup of Joe (coffee), a donut, and headed east on the four lane for central Iowa. They weren't kidding when they called this farm country! Crossed the Missouri, flew by Mitchell, home of the Corn Palace. A lot of work goes into creating those panels each year, all made from corn. Must be a corny place! Ooh bad joke! Hope it was better than my deer crossing joke.

Patrick was only half awake by then, didn't want to see it either. Enter Minnesota. 'HI, Bill, Anne, Dale'. Bill lives in Alaska, don't know where Anne is, and Dale lives near Minneapolis (Names have been change to protect the innocent, the guilty are named out-right, Bill, Anne, Dale. You know in which category you fit).

Shortly after lunch we turn south and enter Iowa. I remind Patrick to watch for farm equipment. They own the road and their top speed is 20. Can't see much of the Iowa countryside. The corn is taller than our vehicle. A silo or a tree every once in a while breaks the corn fields. I'm doing the navigating now. Turn right at the next intersection, in about five miles or so.

Here we are. This is where your Grandmother grew up. Over there was your great, great grandfather's place. All gone now, we've spread out. Doubt any of us will return.

Head into town, have dinner at the motel. Hit the hot tub, a good way to end the day! Breakfast at the coffee shop across the street from the motel. Must be 'senior' day. Most of the folks have more grey hair than me. They all must be regulars, as the waitresses seem to know their names.

Gas the car, and head out. The new four lane goes south of the city. I'm having Patrick drive while the roads are straight. He doesn't need 3 lanes. I'll drive once we get to Illinois. The kid is a good driver, uses the turn signals when changing lanes and all that. I always wondered what that switch was for.

Time to get gas again. We'll take the "Business Route," should be plenty of choices along the way. Humm, 2 miles. Three. Looks more residential than business. There is one on our left. Sort of on an island, but how do we get to it? Left turn across three lanes of traffic, guess I could do it. We have "hick" plates. You know, where I come from, a cow on the road and three cars cause a major headache at "rush hour." (Rush Hour, the time it takes to stop at the cafe, gulp down a cup of coffee, and get home to the missis). Found a truck stop and fueled up there.

Better call Mom and tell her where we were at and what time I (we) expect to get there. Oops, should have called her sooner! She was worrying where we were at and all that other stuff mothers do.

Cross over the "Mighty" Mississippi River and find a place to get some fuel, again. Soda pop and donuts too. (Trips are good for junk food free-for-all).

I take over the driving chores, added some more to the four lane. So that's how they did it. The two west bound lanes are on the north side of the ridge and the east bound are on the south, to put all four lanes next to each other, we'd have to call it "Old flat top!" The east bound lanes are the old highway, still the same old roller coaster ride, down the hill around the corner up the hill, down, up and down again. I used to get sick along this part of the route.

I got directions from one them "online map" companies for this part of the trip. Thinking they might have a short cut. Wilson road becomes Jonson Lane at mile post 143.5 and becomes Pot Hole Boulevard at mile post 154.9, which becomes

Jonson Lane at... Awh why don't they use the highway numbers (that's what they are there for) instead of the local names. HERE, put these in the appropriate spot in the back seat! (You get my meaning). I know this route better than they do. Probably had been driving for a while before the computer geniuses were ever born.

Here is the high school, the junior high, oh excuse me "Middle" school, and the old home. We'll take a better look tomorrow, Mom is probably pacing the floor. Three left turns from the main road, (these are not straight streets), around we go again. I'm missing a street. Ah here it is! Finally! At Mom's at last. Into HER car, it's time for dinner!

After dinner, we get settled in. We get the bedroom and Mom will sleep on the sofa, (as she does quite frequently). We "hit-the-hay" early. It's been an emotionally draining day.

As soon as I stir, Mom is up! "Do you want some orange juice? Have a banana. Do you want some cereal? What are you going to do today? What am I going to tell your brothers? We've got to make plans". Aghhh. Doesn't she know that I have 45 minutes of getting dressed to do?

Well, I thought we would tour the area. Go by the house again and the schools. I'll talk to Patrick when he gets up. We'll let you know before we leave. Looks like we might get some rain. I look at the lake out the kitchen window, while sipping my OJ. Nice, but I miss the mountains of Utah.

We tour the area. I tell Patrick what the area and the schools were like when I went there. We stop and look at the old house and tell him all that we had done. Dormers have been added, they are out of scale. I would have done three and smaller. I also would have looked at other houses in the area to see what they have done. A two story house has been built on the corner. It's totally out of place and dwarfs the neighboring houses.

Some areas had heavy rain, large puddles in the road. Drains must be plugged again. Get home just in time for dinner. Patrick finds the "Scrabble" game. Dear-old-dad can't win for losing. Patrick was the over-all winner. Patrick was always hard to beat at board games. Bed time.

We go over to my brother, Jim's, place for pizza. Patrick fits right in. Just like he had seen his uncles, aunts and cousin all the time. Made me very happy. Got home not too late, did some laundry. Got ready to head back west.

I get up at my usual time and soon "chomping-at-the-bit"! Ready to go but Patrick is a little harder to get motivated. Finally we head out. Going to visit a friend of Patrick's who lives across the state. Patrick and John have a good visit before they roll up the sidewalks at 7pm. We found a nice little motel. The beds are foot to foot. I like it.

After breakfast, we travel the state highways. Heading north and west til we find a little old bridge crossing the Mississippi. SURPRISE! It's a toll bridge, $1.50! We scramble to find correct change. Too early to give them a fifty. If they are raising funds to paint the bridge. They're too late. The rust has taken over. If they are going to replace it, at this rate, it will fall down before they collect enough. That reminds me. We waited for a tug boat on the Illinois River, a swinging bridge. Seemed like it took a long time.

We traveled across Iowa on a US Highway, no need to drive the Interstate, or as some people like to call it "The Trucker's Expressway." Get to see more corn fields up close this way. Don't see Iowa unless you see the corn fields! Actually they do raise other crops and it is a pretty state.

We join up with the Interstate in Nebraska, and basically travel the route of the pioneers, flat wheat land! We missed the museum built over the highway. Doubt Patrick would want to see it.

On to Wyoming. The country is getting dryer, less green and browner. We cross the high plains of southern Wyoming. They tell me they get 10 feet of snow in winter, all of it moving sideways! At Rock Springs, we turn north to Idaho and back to college. Interesting highway, passing lanes about every eight miles. At this time of the year there is hardly any traffic. I wonder if they are needed when the tourists are headed to Yellowstone.

We stop for gas. My son points to a road going up the mountains. I tell him I ain't driving that. He says it's my turn to drive. "Not if you want to go that way. We go on like this for another minute or so. I drive. I was going to drive anyhow, but it was good fun to have this "discussion."

Shoulder construction. The highway department is cleaning out the barrow pits. Stop-n-go and sometime a single lane. Secretly, I glad I'm driving, although Patrick is a good driver. I'm more relaxed when I'm driving through "construction zones" (a mother hen thing or should that be father rooster).

Over the mountains, I stop for a break, will let Patrick drive as he seems to know the way. I called the missis (as I did everyday), will be home tomorrow. I think the grandkids are wearing her out. It has been a long trip for all of us. (music in background, *...another tank of gas and back on the road again...*)

Chapter 10: OFF TO THE REC CENTER

Well I'm off to the rec center. It's a rainy day so I can't do any gardening. The missis says I spend too much time watching the westerns or playing with the trains. I protest, I lose. But I still get the last word in; "Yes Dear".

The missis recently read that people with Parkinson's (PWP) need lots of exercise (she keeps up with that kind of stuff). I remind her of all the exercise I get. I do more than the cat. I protest, I lose. But I still get the last... ah you know.

So, here I am! Lots of handicapped parking. Most of them are already taken! Busy place. I thought seniors slept till noon! I pull in to a spot. Whew! Just missed the other car. Ya think they would make the spots wider. Where's that friend with the flashlights and orange cones when you need him?

The "Rec Center" (actually, Recreation Center). Think it should be "Wreck-re-ation" at least on the senior side. It's a multi-million dollar facility approved by the voters several years ago. The seniors have their own area; exercise room, library, computers, and they even serve lunch. Sometimes it's even good, or so I've been told. I find the exercise room, correction, "Wellness Center".

I've have been doing that a lot lately, correcting myself. New names for old things. Probably the job of some bureaucrat in D.C. to think of these things.

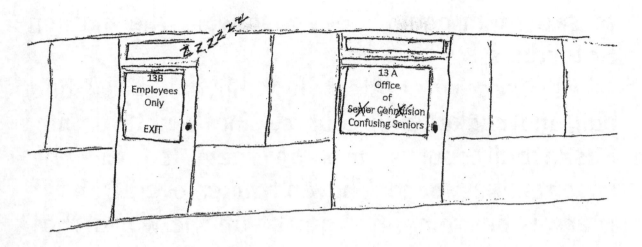

I'm supposed to be telling you about my adventure at the rec center. Oh let's see. Oh yea. I just arrived at the "Wellness" room. Lots of machines; 2 of this type, one of these, 2 of those, 1 of them and I have no idea what half of them do. Where to start? Just then a couple (Do I call them an old couple? They are probably just a few years older than me). Problem solved! They introduce themselves as Mike and Becky.

They suggest I start with the bike, and showed me how the other machines work. Push a button for more weight (later I learned it's called resistance). I go around the room and try all of the machines, pressed one on most, got up to 3 on one, not as strong as I thought. Will have to come back again. Had a good time and good conversation with Mike and Becky. Hope to see them again. They also walk the mall on Saturdays.

Let's see what else they have here. Hand ball and racket ball courts. That's not for me. Basketball courts, lots of them (so far the imports like "soccer" haven't taken over. Don't if there is anything in the rest of the world that comes close). By-golly, the girls are playing with the boys! In my days the girls had their own teams. Bet-ya they don't play 'shirts-n-skins'! Why couldn't we have co-ed teams when I was young?

Running track, better be careful, or I'll get run over. Ah, the sign over there says walking time on the track is from 11 to 12. I'll come back then. As I look around, I see spin cycles. Some of the folks go pretty fast. No wonder the seniors have their own space. Tread mills, stair steppers, and other machines, but most are being used. Zumba (whatever that is) class? Looks like it takes a lot of energy but not for me. Let's check out the pools.

The big pool. Looks like some training going on for a meet, and some people dancing around in one corner. Children play area and water slides! We had nothing like this when I was a kid, a rope and a raft if we lucky. Swam out so far, turned around and came back. Played in the shallow water, and the sun, and sand. Oh. Those sunburns hurt. We didn't have sun screen. A lap pool, holding swimming lessons in it. Hot tub looks inviting!

To the locker room! Twenty minutes later I emerge, a prune in shorts but freshly showered. We always showered before entering a pool. I shuffle down to the hot tub. Ah the water is warm. I settle down. I don't know if the hot tub does any good for PWP, but feels good.

Mike and Becky are there. They tell me that was a water aerobics (exercise) class in the big pool. They suggest I try it. Easy on the bones. I sit in front of one of the jets. It nearly pushes me across the tub! It feels good on the back. I stay in the tub for about twenty minutes. I sit most of the time in the calm water next to the jets. It feels good too.

There is not much you can do in the way of exercise, so I people watch. A group of teenage boys run by. They have lean tight bodies now but what will they look like in 20 years? A young lady walks by. She is a knockout, mid 20's I'd say. OOPS, she is a mother of 3 girls. Make that early 30's. Wonder how she keeps her shape? Speaking of shape, two gray hair ladies enter the hot tub. Water level will probably go up 3 inches. Uh-oh, this guy's belly hangs over his trunks by at least by 4 inches. Glad I don't look that way! A group of teenage girls, giggling and such go by. They like the boys. I wonder what they will look like in 20 years.

The young children like the water slides and the babies like splashing in the shallow water. You see all kinds of shapes while sitting in the hot tub. If I looked like some of them, I wouldn't leave of the house.

Time to go. Say good bye to Mike and Becky, and head for the locker room. Darn, missed the track time. WHATS THIS?? The missis is walking towards me! She has a fine shape for a lady of her age. We go back to the hot tub and I introduce her to Mike and Becky. The girls start chatting away like old friends. Mike and I go back to girl wat.., I mean, people watching. Think I'll come again, maybe even on a sunny day.

Chapter 11: I HAVE PARKINSON'S DISEASE

I have Parkinson's Disease (PD). It has affected every aspect of my life, and hopefully, my stories have helped you to understand a little bit about what life is for me, and others with PD. There is no known cure yet, although some herbals can help.

It has also affected the life of my lovely, understanding late wife and my kids. Hopefully my stories have been amusing and have given a little hope that having PD is not the end of the world.

In advances stages, it's not easy for people to miss. Most people understand. Some people want to help, where help is not needed, but still appreciated. And sometimes, I need help when none is around, but as we ALL do in life (healthy or not), we make do. If you have P.D. don't be offended by offers of help.

This work is not intended to be a complaining session. Sure, I'm not happy about having PD, but there are worse things as well, so I'm happy to be alive!! Hey, my friend is deaf and he suffers from that as well.

This book is probably going to be my final achievement of any notice, and I'm proud of it and if it helps one person understand PD a little better then it is a success!

Thanks to my late wife, who supported me through the experiences and for being patient with me when it took me 4 times as long to fix the faucet or vacuum the floor.

If you discover that you have PD, don't give up and think that life is over. It's a matter of finding ways to compensate, just as the painter that paints with their feet because they have no hands (actually that would be pretty cool. I can't paint with my hands even! – unless you like abstract art). Just like in the Clint Eastwood movie "Heartbreak Ridge", we have to "adjust, adapt, and overcome" (I don't remember the exact words, but I'm close).

Sincerely, Steven Briggs

ACKNOWLEDGMENTS

I do want to thank my family and friends for their support and my friend, Anthony, that helped me publish this work.

Printed in the United States
By Bookmasters